"This generation of Christians [...] only biblical revelation about re[...] Questions for Restless Minds series poses many of the toughest questions faced by young Christians to some of the world's foremost Christian thinkers and leaders. Along the way, this series seeks to help the Christian next generation to learn how to think biblically when they face questions in years to come that perhaps no one yet sees coming."

—**Russell Moore,**
public theologian, *Christianity Today*

"This is a well-written, well-documented, and very important book on a major concern in society and the church today. Abuse and trauma are nothing new, of course, but they have become rampant. This book can help the church understand and become active in helping those who are victims of this very heartbreaking epidemic. The authors masterfully combine the empirical, scientific, statistical, and clinical data with careful articulation of biblical and theological truth about the realities of life as fallen and corrupt people in a fallen and corrupt world. God has done his work to redeem us for now and eternity through Jesus Christ, and this includes those who have suffered severe abuse and trauma. The church needs to be fully active in reaching out to meet abused and traumatized people where they are with God's love and grace."

—**Richard E. Averbeck,**
professor of Old Testament and Semitic languages,
Trinity Evangelical Divinity School

"Profound, insightful, compassionate, and practical. This book weaves together the latest scientific and professional knowledge about psychological trauma and abuse with deep theological and pastoral wisdom. The complementary backgrounds of the authors provide a unique, cohesive, and authentically Christian perspective on these critically important topics. Essential reading for pastors and Christian lay-people who wish to support the many victims of abuse within our congregations."

—John Wyatt,
Emeritus Professor of Neonatal Pediatrics,
University College, London;
president of the Christian Medical Fellowship

How Can We Help Victims of Trauma and Abuse?

Questions for Restless Minds

Questions for Restless Minds

QUESTIONS FOR RESTLESS MINDS

How Can We Help Victims of Trauma and Abuse?

**Susan L. and
Stephen N. Williams**

D. A. Carson,
Series Editor

LEXHAM PRESS

How Can We Help Victims of Trauma and Abuse?
Questions for Restless Minds, edited by D. A. Carson

Copyright 2021 Christ on Campus Initiative

Lexham Press, 1313 Commercial St., Bellingham, WA 98225
LexhamPress.com

Print ISBN 9781683595113
Digital ISBN 9781683595120
Library of Congress Control Number 2021937711

Lexham Editorial: Todd Hains, Abigail Stocker, Danielle Thevenaz, Mandi Newell
Cover Design: Brittany Schrock
Typesetting: Abigail Stocker

The Christ on Campus Initiative exists to inspire students on college and university campuses to think wisely, act with conviction, and become more Christlike by providing relevant and excellent evangelical resources on contemporary issues.

Visit christoncampuscci.org.

TRINITY
EVANGELICAL DIVINITY SCHOOL
TRINITY INTERNATIONAL UNIVERSITY

Contents

Series Preface

D. A. CARSON, SERIES EDITOR

T HE ORIGIN OF this series of books lies with a group of faculty from Trinity Evangelical Divinity School (TEDS), under the leadership of Scott Manetsch. We wanted to address topics faced by today's undergraduates, especially those from Christian homes and churches.

If you are one such student, you already know what we have in mind. You know that most churches, however encouraging they may be, are not equipped to prepare you for what you will face when you enroll at university.

It's not as if you've never known any winsome atheists before going to college; it's not as if you've never thought about Islam, or the credibility of the New Testament documents, or the nature of friendship, or gender identity, or how the claims of Jesus sound too exclusive and rather narrow, or the nature of evil. But up until now you've probably thought about such things within the shielding cocoon of a community of faith.

Now you are at college, and the communities in which you are embedded often find Christian perspectives to be at best oddly quaint and old-fashioned, if not repulsive. To use the current jargon, it's easy to become socialized into a new community, a new world.

How shall you respond? You could, of course, withdraw a little: just buckle down and study computer science or Roman history (or whatever your subject is) and refuse to engage with others. Or you could throw over your Christian heritage as something that belongs to your immature years and buy into the cultural package that surrounds you. Or—and this is what we hope you will do—you could become better informed.

But how shall you go about this? On any disputed topic, you do not have the time, and probably not the interest, to bury yourself in a couple of dozen volumes written by experts for experts. And if you did, that would be on *one* topic—and there are scores of topics that will grab the attention of the inquisitive student. On the other hand, brief pamphlets with predictable answers couched in safe slogans will prove to be neither attractive nor convincing.

So we have adopted a middle course. We have written short books pitched at undergraduates who want arguments that are accessible and stimulating, but invariably courteous. The material is comprehensive enough that it has become an important resource for pastors and other campus leaders who devote their energies to work with students. Each book ends with a brief annotated bibliography and study questions, intended for readers who want to probe a little further.

Lexham Press is making this series available both as attractive books and digitally in new formats (ebook and Logos resource). We hope and pray you will find them helpful and convincing.

1

INTRODUCTION

"TRAUMA" AND "ABUSE": two dark words that describe the experience of a vast number of devastated people throughout the world. Unless we rightly understand the psychospiritual impact of this ordeal, our Christian response, however good-hearted, may not be helpful. What we think *is* helpful for non-professionals, is to acquire an understanding of the multi-dimensional impact of trauma. So we are giving time to describe the experience of the trauma of abuse. If we set out our task in terms of description and theological reflection, it may sound clinical and callous. Right from the outset, both authors wish to distance themselves from this attitude. Susan Williams's counseling in the area of trauma and wrestling with its psychospiritual impact is the outcome of her personal immersion in that world. Stephen Williams's involvement is the result of seeking to think with her through the implications of that world in the light of Christian faith. Our aim is to bring understanding where ignorance can be seriously damaging both to individuals who are not understood and to the whole body of Christ, where the disconnections caused by traumatic wounding make us corporately less than we are destined to be as "the fullness of Him who fills all in all" (Eph 1:23 ESV).[1] We do not want to end up where people like T. S. Eliot ended up: "All our knowledge brings us nearer to our ignorance / All our ignorance brings us nearer to death / But nearness to death no nearer to God."[2] The experiential world of trauma and abuse is much darker than these two words connote for those who have not experienced them, but there is a Light that no darkness will ever extinguish and a Life in him that death cannot destroy.

WHAT IS TRAUMA?

TRAUMA (τραύμα) IS a Greek word, meaning "wound." It occurs once in the New Testament in the story usually called the parable of the Good Samaritan where it refers to the wounds of the assault victim whom he helped (Luke 10:34). Apparently, the word "trauma" in English did not come to mean a psychological wound until the 1890s.[3] We are adopting this usage and so not dealing with trauma in the sense referred to in a "trauma center" in major hospitals, where skilled medical practitioners provide specialist care for the most severely injured patients. Psychological trauma can be part of the experience of these severely injured patients, but those who suffer abuse with no major physical trauma (e.g., inappropriate sexual touching) are just as likely to experience psychological trauma with all its enduring consequences, including flashbacks and intrusive thoughts about the trauma and overpowering avoidance of certain aspects of the experience; they are easily startled, on edge, and have trouble concentrating and sleeping.

There is no hard and fast distinction between the psychological and physical implications of trauma. The relation of the mind to the brain has long been a contentious subject, but however we understand it, the physical brain is clearly affected by psychological trauma.[4] The impact on the brain simply of remembering an overwhelming event can be observed using technology such as magnetic resonance imaging (MRI). This technology is being continually refined through advances in neuroscience to give us increasingly detailed images of brain trauma caused without physical force.[5] When this impact is enduring, the neurophysiological consequences of trauma can be life-changing. For example, the amygdala (which is the threat detector in the brain) becomes hyperreactive so the traumatized person often feels on red alert. Every time the amygdala is triggered, it shuts down higher brain functions to focus on preparing for fight or flight. Yet those are the very functions that help with making wise judgments and good choices. In addition, the corrosive effect on the hippocampus of chronic stimulation of stress hormones leaves survivors[6] of repeated sexual abuse with neurological damage to the brain hardware that stores this memory, sometimes resulting in learning deficits that vex them for life.[7]

Other posttraumatic changes in the brain can affect the heart, blood pressure, and the autoimmune system, significantly damaging health. An otherwise very healthy man who was a teenager when his father was brutally murdered by a car bomb during "the Troubles" in Northern Ireland had to have a pacemaker implanted in his heart not long after his thirtieth birthday. There are also numerous examples of various types of arthritis in young victims of trauma, including former soldiers and extreme abuse survivors. In this way the impact of psychological trauma is indirectly physical. We therefore must not falsely spiritualize psychological trauma any more than we would falsely spiritualize the physical condition of an earthquake victim with broken limbs. Psychospiritual damage is thoroughly embodied. Any account of trauma that ignores this is reductionistic.

With or without life-threatening wounds to the body, the impact of a traumatic event catapults the survivor into an alien world of psychospiritual pain. If such an event occurs when a person is old enough to notice change, everything suddenly looks in some indefinable way altered by the unfathomable distress. The control seat at the very center of your lived experience, the observer self through whom you perceive and interpret the world, has been bizarrely transmuted in ways which cast an unfamiliar light on all of life, suffusing posttraumatic experience with the sense of being a wounded stranger in a strange world, a world often encountered as hostile, enemy territory because of the enduring resonance of unassuaged terror. The global loss of the safe and familiar world, including the familiar self and self-control, amount to a radical unmaking of the lived world of the traumatized. The intense yearning for normality, to return to the time before trauma, coexists with uncontrollable memories erupting into conscious life as a consequence of such things as nightmares, images, and sensory or emotional memories.

Most of this also applies to those too young to remember a time before their traumatic experience, but for children the traumatic impact of abuse is compounded since they are inherently more vulnerable and helpless. There may be no "normality" to return to. Instead, traumatized children will create their own kind of stable "normality" out of the materials in their often severely limited social environment, which can be more destructive than life-enhancing. The ways that caregivers deal with their own emotions become models for the ways that children learn to manage their own emotional distress. When caregivers silence their own emotions and avoid their emotional needs, children also learn to silence their own emotions and to avoid their emotional needs. And when caregivers use addictions to soothe their own emotional distress rather than seeking comfort from others or through pleasant diversions such as music or nature, children also learn that addictions are a necessary way of managing emotional needs. Thus, the very world that traumatizes children also shapes them in the ways they cope with their emotional distress in the future. We will explore this further when we look at some of the defenses children use to contain distressing emotions they cannot regulate.

Under these circumstances, emotions (which are the initial communicators of a person's inner world) are quelled before they can begin to be expressed. Nevertheless, emotional fragments may break loose, as it were, from the memory of the event that created them, still conveying distress in the form of an emotional memory. This is particularly painful and bewildering, like living in the heart of an emotional volcano with no context for understanding where you are or why you are there. The fact that this emotional information is not only urgent but explosively unprocessed means that the body is puppeteered without the victim's knowing why he or she is not really in control. This powerlessness over the posttraumatic internal world makes a mockery of any resolve to find solid ground. It can be as challenging for the traumatized to get a grip on the psychological consequences of trauma as on the overwhelming experience of the traumatic event itself with its own shocking sensory and emotional data. A sense of utter helplessness already stamped on the soul of a survivor by the overpowering event is stamped even deeper by these overpowering emotional consequences.

3

WHAT IS
ABUSE?

A BUSE IS ONE of the experiences that can cause trauma. It can take a number of different forms. When we encounter the word "abuse," we normally think of it in physical terms, often specifically sexual. It goes without saying that we keep this in mind.[8] However, there is a wider, frequently neglected sense. All forms of abuse have an emotional dimension, but the abuser who repeatedly silences, demeans, humiliates, undermines, manipulates, coerces, or deceives a person inflicts emotional abuse. Naturally, this comes in degrees as well as kinds and not every example we can think of from the list above should be stretched to fit the term "emotional abuse." However, such patterns of behavior can be abusive on a horrendous scale with devastating consequences.

The UK Serious Crime Act of 2015 makes behavior that is persistently "coercive or controlling behaviour against an intimate partner or family member" punishable by a prison term of up to five years.[9] Whatever we think of this sentence or various applications of the law, the Act rightly indicates the seriousness of the behavior. Coercive behavior is understood in this context as "a pattern of acts of assault, threats, humiliation and intimidation or other abuse that is used to harm, punish, or frighten their victim" which bridges the physical and nonphysical aspects of abuse.[10]

The introduction of this legislation reflected a wider public awareness of the extreme harm caused by emotional abuse, which was also reflected in themes treated in popular BBC soaps at the time. On June 17, 2017, the British newspaper *The Independent* published an article revealing that reports of child emotional abuse had surged 200% in seven years amid cuts to child protection services. The subtitle reads: "'Devastating' rise in reports of parents telling their children they hate them or wish they were dead." North American statistics for child maltreatment are just as disheartening, though they fail to show the full scale of the problem. The SPCC (Society for the Positive Care of Children) website admits that the reporting of emotional abuse is hampered by ignorance of what exactly belongs in that category, indicating that more work is needed to raise awareness before the extent of emotional abuse can even be assessed.

Emotional abuse occurs when people are repeatedly silenced at home, given no chance to voice their needs either verbally or through emotions, and treated as though or told that they are unloved. The impact of additional emotional abuse, such as being bullied in the public sphere—bullies often sense the vulnerability of the emotionally abused—increases the sense of devastation. Tragically, a grim cycle often characterizes the lives of the abused. The monumental Adverse Childhood Experiences (ACE) study from the Centers for Disease Control (CDC) in Atlanta showed that "women who had an early history of abuse and neglect were seven times more likely to be raped in adulthood."[11] Childhood trauma thus carries with it a higher likelihood of accumulating traumatic experiences during the course of a lifetime.

As Christians, we need to be aware of the spiritual suffering that inevitably follows emotional abuse. While physical or sexual abuse is obvious to the victim, emotional abuse is much less obvious and easily infiltrates relationships in the church that are meant to model the noncoercive love of Jesus. Yet it is often not even on our radar. When the abused hear Paul and Peter modeling non-coercive respect for others (2 Cor 9:7; Phlm 14; 1 Pet 5:2) they can often barely hear these apostolic voices as non-coercive. Where emotional trauma leaves a legacy of terror in an inner world that feels locked in helpless isolation, the sense of the presence of God is banished. If we have been subject to emotional abuse, we may conclude that God is not there, because our experience of life is of the emotional absence of anyone meant to care for us. Alternatively, we may conclude that God is there but not willing to help, because that is how we have experienced the presence of those meant to be there to help. Or again, we may conclude that God is there, but that he is a terrifying presence, because we continue in God's presence to experience the posttraumatic emotional memory of terror.

Traumatic experience is often made up of a number of perplexing strands that must be disentangled. Each strand is significant because accumulation of abuse means accumulation of traumatic (di)stress. A single rape is seriously traumatic. Being trapped in a relationship where rape is a persistent, if unpredictable, feature of life brings wave after wave of horror, affording no space between events for the safety needed to begin the process of healing. Abuse is often multifaceted. It can take either a conspicuous or a subtle form. For example, the violation of personal boundaries, conspicuous in the case of physical abuse, occurs more subtly in emotional abuse which diminishes a person's sense of ownership over his or her own body; this often paves the way for more explicitly abusive violations of the body's boundaries. Our contemporary lack of social consensus on sexual ethics and cultural obsession with erotic sexuality complicate the question of relational boundaries. What counts as violation and victimhood may be unclear. In our supposedly shame-free society, sexual violation nevertheless brings a shame that defies the "anything goes" culture, a culture that makes the shame puzzling. Disentangling the threads of abuse is further complicated by the subtle nature of incremental abuse as it moves from the psychological to the physical dimension—a common progression.

Those who are traumatized can be overwhelmed by the complexity of their experience. The enormity of just one aspect of abuse can blind them to other, hidden layers of experience. The physical harm caused by sexual abuse varies but sometimes it is overlooked in its own right because there is a focus on the sexual component. Further, emotional pain is intensified with the shattering of belief about the person who is actually causing harm, especially when this is the one who is meant to protect the victim from such harm. When the victim is deprived of a sense of safety in her or his own home, the basis for flourishing becomes radically insecure. If the perpetrator of abuse was in a trusted relationship with the victim, the betrayal of trust constitutes another facet of the abuse that the victim must work through. If someone in a position of spiritual authority commits the abuse, then a form of spiritual abuse is also involved with an attendant impact on the survivor's capacity to trust anyone in spiritual authority in the future. Each aspect of abuse accumulates stressors, so that the more facets of abuse someone experiences, the more stressful the abuse becomes, and the greater the overall stress load, the more likely it is that the capacity of the traumatized person to cope will break down.

With each stressor entailed in a traumatic experience, losses are incurred. In major event trauma, losses are often blatant consequences of the event, for example, disability, bereavement, loss of a home. But all too often the hidden losses of abuse go unrecognized. People who are abused feel their very being is made "defective" in some extraordinary way by the abuse and it cannot be made right. While our sinfulness is a defect common to all of us, this posttraumatic defectiveness is experienced as personally unique, something which marks out the traumatized individual as a thoroughly deplorable person, beneath contempt from any point of view, even God's. How can we measure the loss of a sense of a healthy, "undefective" self? Or the loss of the sense of well-being associated with a safe world? Trauma is a subtle as well as a blatant evil. The evil is accentuated when a child is involved.

4

CHILDHOOD TRAUMA

BEFORE EXPLORING FURTHER implications of trauma, we must note the crucial distinction between child and adult trauma. Speaking on behalf of his colleagues in the field of trauma, Bessel van der Kolk said: "We all were familiar with the basics of how trauma affects the developing mind and brain, and we all were aware that childhood trauma is radically different from traumatic stress in adults."[12] Where the abuse victim is a child, he or she is often described by traumatologists as suffering from *developmental trauma*. Among clinicians, this basic fact about the distinctive impact of developmental trauma has become axiomatic. Since the brain and body of the victim are still developing when the neurophysiological damage occurs, trauma not only causes the typical devastation of traumatic stress but also disrupts development at the particular stage when it occurs. A child is thus impacted in ways peculiar both to the event itself and to the growing brain at that developmental stage. Although all trauma is profoundly personal, impacting survivors in highly individualized ways, there are common patterns of experience that we can categorize and that make developmental trauma distinctively damaging.

"Early maltreatment has enduring negative effects on brain development. Our brains are sculpted by our early experiences. Maltreatment is a chisel that shapes a brain to contend with strife, but at the cost of deep enduring wounds."[13] The notion of "maltreatment" introduces another dimension of abuse, particularly in relation to children. When children's needs are not met, this is a form of maltreatment. If physical needs are neglected, such as when children are starved or abandoned in a house on their own when they are too young to fend for themselves, it is normally classed as abuse. Equally, when children are emotionally neglected or deprived, the psychological impact is very similar to that of abuse, though we may stop short of referring to emotional deprivation as abuse when parents are truly well-intentioned since their own limitations (e.g., emotional damage or mental illness) have made them unable to provide for their children's emotional needs.

When any of these forms of trauma occurs in childhood, crucial developmental milestones are potentially missed, leaving children with significant problems regulating emotions, concentrating, and building successful relationships in later life. Potentially, there are also distinctive epigenetic implications.[14] It is as important to know the age at which an event has occurred as it is to know the actual nature of the event. Those of us who work with trauma survivors discover a huge disparity in the recovery trajectory of those adults who have no childhood trauma history and those whose adult trauma is grafted onto earlier developmental trauma.

It should also be noted that "secondary trauma" can occur when children are indirectly traumatized by their parents' traumatic experiences. This can be transmitted through the fear communicated to the child through the body, behavior, or wider emotional patterns in the parent's life. Parents who are unable to cope with their own post-traumatic emotions find it difficult to tolerate their child's unprocessed emotions, much less to manage their crucial responsibility to help their children learn to regulate their emotions. They will struggle to be attuned to their child's emotional states and may even be terrified by the lack of control over both their own and their child's emotions. This can lead to emotional and even physical abuse in attempts to block out the effect of the child's negative emotions. The fact that the overwhelming majority of abused children are abused in their first year conjures up the scene of emotionally damaged parents utterly out of control when their baby cries.

Newborn babies have no capacity for regulating their emotions. Without help, the impact of stress hormones on a baby's brain can be so toxic that the child will automatically shut down emotionally, deploying a protective defense mechanism to avoid brain damage.[15] But there is collateral damage: the capacity to feel more generally is thwarted. Since our emotions are fundamentally an internal communication system whereby we convey information to ourselves about the meaning and significance of experience, incapacity to feel means we lose connection with ourselves. Consequently, when the traumatized grow beyond childhood, they fail to grasp a sense of the meaningfulness of their own lives or the significance of thoughts or events and are understandably unable to sustain healthy or intimate relationships (which rely on emotional attunement) or to make good choices. Yet in spite of this numbing of some emotions, trauma survivors can feel unassuaged guilt, shame, terror, mistrust, or alienation along with utter aloneness and hopelessness. Suicidal thoughts, substance abuse, or other addictions often seem to offer the only hope of reprieve.

The extent of child abuse and its implications are staggering. In relation to levels in the United States, Bessel van der Kolk wrote:

> The first time I heard Robert Anda, MD, present the results of the ACE [Adverse Childhood Experiences] study, he could not hold back his tears. In his career at the CDC he had previously worked in several major risk areas. ... But when the ACE study data started to appear on his computer screen, he realized that they had stumbled upon the gravest and most costly public health issue in the United States: child abuse. He had calculated that its overall costs exceeded those of cancer or heart disease and that eradicating child abuse in America would reduce the overall rate of depression by more than half, alcoholism by two-thirds,

and suicide, IV drug use and domestic violence by three-quarters. It would also have a dramatic effect on workplace performance and vastly decrease the need for incarceration.[16]

Even these facts fail to cover the full extent of the tragedy. Who can measure the magnitude of more hidden losses, such as the precious gift of childhood innocence— that innocence which allows us to live our early days in a world of apparent goodness, where beauty is unalloyed by the ugliness of evil or lovelessness, where play can magically recreate a paradise lost, and where trust is straightforward and natural? When a child's capacity to trust is broken, when there is no sense of the real possibility of paradise, of a love that can be trusted, a barrier is formed within that can prevent the sufferer from receiving the right help from anyone.

5

MAJOR IMPLICATIONS OF TRAUMATIC ABUSE

H AVING TRIED TO indicate both the distinction and the
unity between childhood and adult trauma, we now turn
to an overview of four of the wider implications of abuse.
The discussion of the fourth will lead us to the issues traumatic abuse raises for faith.

THE SHATTERING
OF CORE BELIEFS

Trauma can shatter the very foundations of our beliefs. For
the sake of simplicity, we distinguish between conscious
and unconscious beliefs or assumptions about the world
and ourselves. Traumatic experience has the power to strip
off the plasterboard of our conscious beliefs. Unconscious
beliefs previously buried beneath them instantaneously
come to light. Janoff-Bulman gives an example:

> We generally operate on the basis of an illusion of
> invulnerability, a basic belief that "it can't happen
> to me." We may intellectually maintain that one out
> of four people gets cancer and that crimes and car
> accidents are common. Yet we truly do not believe
> that these events will happen to us. Work by per-
> sonality theorists and object relations theorists sug-
> gests that this sense of safety and security may be

35

fundamental to the healthy personality and is first developed very early in childhood through responsible, predictable interactions with caregivers. ... The coping task facing victims is largely a difficult cognitive dilemma; they must integrate the data of their dramatic, negative experience and their prior assumptions, which cannot readily assimilate the new information. Victims must rework the new data so as to make it fit and thereby maintain their old assumptions, or they must revise their old assumptions in a way that precludes the breakdown of the entire system and allows them to perceive the world as not wholly threatening.[17]

If, for instance, a traumatic event shatters your belief in God's love, your whole Christian belief system may well seem irreparable or your concept of God may become much more impersonal. Unless you construct understandings that genuinely make sense in the light of your traumatic experience, faith becomes a façade.

RUNAWAY EMOTIONS

After a traumatic experience, the explosion of powerful new emotions makes the trauma victim feel like someone saddled, without warning, on the back of a bucking bronco. Because traumatic experience wreaks havoc with your capacity to process and regulate emotions, these emotions become incomprehensible. For example, your body gives every indication of experiencing fear because you suddenly start to run away or hide behind a door. Yet there is no apparent reason for what can seem like bizarre behavior, which can be puzzling and embarrassing. Anger can boil up in a flash and you may not have a clue why. On top of the fear and anxiety which came from the horrifying trauma, you can feel alarmed at the seismic power of your feelings, terrified that they will run away with you and destroy your world, like greased pigs in a garden of priceless orchids. Persons suffering from PTSD (Posttraumatic Stress Disorder) may "experience just having feelings as being dangerous. Because of their difficulty in using emotions to help them think through situations and come up with adaptive solutions, emotions merely become reminders of their inability to affect the outcome of their life."[18]

We noted earlier that emotions constitute our most primitive communication system. Babies communicate through them long before they can use words. Caregivers gradually help them interpret those embodied signals of distress or well-being, ultimately with increasingly specific verbal descriptions.[19] This is how we learn to process emotions as we grow. When they are not processed, they generate a multitude of woes since they lack the integrated connections with higher brain functions such as narrative and verbal understanding, which help to moderate painful feeling states or inhibit inappropriate behavior. Distressing emotional memories triggered by images, smells, sounds, sensations, etc., can suddenly invade a person's consciousness when nothing in the context of these emotional memories tells sufferers how to interpret them. Physical aches and pains regularly occur when explicit memory systems have had to be shut down by defenses to cope with the trauma of abuse, so that implicit emotional memory communicates distress through the body without giving an explanation to the conscious mind.[20] The body tells the story of painful trauma but is often only met with pain-relieving drugs.

Understandably, this unprocessed emotion will wreak havoc in relationships. For example, coercive or bullying actions are often attempts to resolve feelings of power-lessness stemming from unprocessed trauma. The person on the receiving end of this coercion has little or no idea of the sense of helplessness that motivated the behavior—the perpetrator certainly does not appear to be helpless to the person on the receiving end! Another example occurs when people manipulatively saddle others with unreason-able expectations, often attempting to meet unresolved emotional needs within themselves for the parental care they failed to receive as children. Parents normally put their young child's needs at the forefront of their lives, whereas an adult who expects his or her needs to be similarly pri-oritized would be considered unreasonable.

The difficulty with regulating emotions is compounded exponentially when the trauma occurs in childhood, since the child has not developed the capacity for self-regulation and is still dependent on adults for help. We have already noted that unregulated emotion is more toxic to the developing brain than to the adult brain. Yet in both cases something kicks in to help cope with these overwhelming emotions. Unknown to the victim, this something comes with a serious health warning, even though it crucially buys time to prepare for the long haul of processing traumatic experience. The "something" we are talking about here is the coping mechanism of psychological defenses.

DEFENSES

Psychological defenses function only if they are hidden. Fundamentally, our defenses distort unwelcome reality, but if we can see that happening, we will no longer believe the version of reality presented by the defenses.[21] We have to believe that version for the defenses to work, and they need to work to offer much-needed protection against the unwelcome reality. This hiddenness makes the distortions very difficult to challenge, like trying to contend with Harry Potter's invisibility cloak. These distortions should not be construed as merely negative phenomena. The overwhelmed brain uses this innate autonomic mechanism for surviving and coping by erasing reality. Only so can stress levels be prevented from causing mental implosion and disabling people altogether in the aftermath of trauma. They buy crucial time for getting on with daily life after the trauma, while processing facts either about the world or the

39

self. These facts can be profoundly threatening to the basic understandings of reality through which people interpret their worlds, and therefore must be integrated gradually.

The most primitive defenses are denial and avoidance, which makes them the first option for children. There is no conscious choice involved here to deny the reality in question or to perpetrate a lie. As the defensive operation is hidden, so the reality that produced it is hidden from the victim. For instance, the abuse victim will often simply deny the abuse actually happened or that the acts actually constituted abuse. It can take years, often within the safety of a therapeutic relationship, for the person to be ready to break down the denial, retrieve the memories, and process the overwhelming reality.

Some emotions are inappropriate or dangerous for a child to experience, such as the terror of abandonment, rage—perhaps even hatred—toward an inadequate caregiver, or sexual pleasure during abuse. Such feelings must be unconsciously repressed until they can be acknowledged and processed. "Many feelings ... were held back because it was not safe to feel them whilst you were a child, so dependent on the parent to regulate you and keep you alive."[22] This defensive maneuver is therefore crucial for survival. When the parent does not help the child to regulate emotion, children "have to find some way to hold themselves together and this is done defensively. Then they attempt to go through life using these defensive strategies, permanently cut off from the flow of mutual regulation with others."[23] The emotional help we are meant to receive from others is blocked. Here is the health warning to which we referred earlier: what may be necessary as a relatively short-term strategy for survival hinders wholesome development in the long run.

A very complex form of defense is dissociation, with a range of ramifications that vary widely in different individuals with different experiences. Someone can have a sense of what is called "derealization," where a traumatic event seems unreal, not really happening or not happening to oneself. This can work in league with denial. Another person's perceptions or thoughts about events that are taking place can be detached from any feelings subconsciously associated with those thoughts and perceptions. Early on in his incarceration in Dachau, one of the Nazi death camps, Bruno Bettelheim realized that his personality had changed; there was a "split within me into one who observed and one to whom things happened."[24] This split can happen instantaneously in the midst of a traumatic event in order to save the hapless victim from being overwhelmed by all the dimensions and meaning of the suffering. This is at the lesser end of the spectrum of dissociation.

A more enduring and pervasive split occurs, particularly with primary-school-aged children, when one or more distinct personality structures with separate identities and self-awareness, often personalized with names, develop within one and the same person. These structurally separate parts of the personality are sometimes called "alters," although sufferers often prefer simply to call them "parts." (These parts should never be assumed to be demons, which well-meaning Christians sometimes unfortunately do.) This level of structural dissociation is referred to as Dissociative Identity Disorder (DID) in the American Psychiatric Association's *Diagnostic and Statistical Manual of Mental Disorders* (DSM-5). Structural dissociation is profound as this may mean that the part of the person who must face the world and take responsibility for all the tasks of everyday life has no memory of the trauma experience. Parts can carry either a particular memory of the experience of extreme deprivation and abuse, an emotion, or a coping capacity for facing the daily demands of life including the regulation of emotions. These parts can also have more apparently destructive roles such as self-punishment, particularly where the victim believed, sometimes through brainwashing, that he or she was in fact the evil one guilty of the offenses that were committed.

While separate personality structures can assist survival in extreme circumstances by preventing emotional overload and meltdown, a multiplicity of personality parts is obviously capable of causing chaotic disruptions in daily life. For instance, making decisions can be maddening when two or more unintegrated value systems collide and make harmony impossible. With structural dissociation, children can, for the most part, live externally normal lives and develop psychologically within personality structures unencumbered by the painful knowledge of their massive trauma, while other parts carry the pain and often fail to develop. Adults can consistently maintain high levels of performance in their jobs, all the while carrying within them child parts that have never developed, so that on a given day one and the same adult may not even know how to read.

This level of dissociation is regularly associated with trauma such as extreme abuse by organized criminal gangs, mercenaries using child soldiers, or satanic ritualists. Yet even with more commonplace experiences like severe emotional deprivation and neglect in children of emotionally and relationally debilitated or mentally unwell parents, structural dissociation involving periodic memory loss can occur. Where the dissociation does not amount to the generation of fully-formed personalities with distinct identities and memories that are unknown to the other parts, the sufferer may still possess a sense of self-division which involves extreme self-loathing, conflicting beliefs, and a lack of adequate self-awareness.

In satanic ritual abuse (SRA), children and adults can be forced to commit vile acts and participate in rituals such as satanic marriage, burial, and sacrifice. Though actual prevalence is impossible to gauge, evidence of this hidden phenomenon is more prevalent than many realize.[25] On September 15, 1989, the Los Angeles County Commission for Women submitted its Report of the Ritual Abuse Task Force. However, it was unable to make much headway because juries found the stories difficult to believe and much of the police evidence disappeared from files.[26]

Because of this, as well as the terror of reprisals if victims speak about their suffering, SRA is largely hidden from the public gaze.[27] Most victims have experienced threats either to their own lives or those of loved ones. When they have also actually witnessed these crimes being carried out against others, their terror is justifiably compounded. The hiddenness of these crimes and the apparent unbelievability of their stories make "coming out" all the more threatening to survivors. While some of the data is hotly contested, those who work with survivors can attest to the unmistakable coherence and consistency of their accounts.[28]

When a survivor later comes to Christian faith or moves in that direction, memories and reactions attached to distinct parts reside alongside the part with no conscious knowledge of the trauma, all within one person at the same time. To build a relationship of trust and understanding with the survivor, the parts have to be approached separately as they reveal themselves, each on its own terms. The terror of the intolerable experience sustains this dissociated fragmentation of the self. However, as different parts speak to a person who can listen to the horrifying story, the intolerable gradually becomes tolerable enough for the survivor to speak the previously unspeakable accounts of past and current experience. Integration is inconceivably difficult and painful to achieve, even through the therapeutic process, but therapists are often richly blessed by these "splendid" people who have suffered so terribly.[29] Friesen rightly uses this perhaps unexpected word because people with DID are often very loving and trustworthy and show remarkable courage in the face of what they have experienced, sometimes with luminous faith in God that defies the darkness that has stolen parts of their lives.

Another form of defense is idealization. Faced with the experience of complete helplessness, the victim invests a caregiver—the very person who may, in fact, be abusive or failing to help—with God-like qualities capable of saving his or her life. In their helplessness, victims can thus attain a kind of vicarious sense of power, as in the phenomenon widely known as "Stockholm Syndrome." It was so named after a bank raid in 1973 where members of the staff were taken hostage for six days; they subsequently refused to testify against their captors because they had developed a psychological dependency on them to cope with the stress of powerlessness. Idealization is a normal part of infancy and childhood when there is no trauma involved; it usually breaks down naturally in adolescence when teenagers suddenly regard their parents as hopelessly inadequate, only to arrive at a more balanced view by the time they make it to their twenties or thirties. But when the child has been traumatically stressed, if only by emotional absence and deprivation, early defensive idealization is often not organically extinguished in adolescence. No typical adolescent rebellion may occur. More blatant trauma, such as physical abuse, can make idealization hard to sustain, especially if there is at least one caregiver who can provide a safe sanctuary for truthful processing.

But where idealization persists, usually alongside contradictory beliefs about the person idealized, then the child's representation of and reaction to the idealized parent can be introjected as a permanent part of his or her personality.[30] This can mean that the toxic style of emotional regulation experienced in childhood—silencing, trivializing, mocking, denigrating, shaming, blaming—is retained within the growing child as an introjected part of the personality, thus perpetuating childhood emotional abuse throughout adulthood in the form of self-abuse. Even publicly or apparently powerful men and women can be hiding a world of debilitatingly hateful self-talk behind their façade of self-assurance.[31]

The defenses to which we have referred are typically regarded as "autonomic"; they operate as automatically as the pumping of the heart or blinking of the eyes. Yet their hidden power to control the internal world causes a deep sense of helplessness that can diminish the person's sense of free or responsible agency. The task of dismantling these powerful defenses in recovery from trauma is herculean because the victim's own sense of agency is needed to deal with the hidden phenomena but is stymied by those very defenses. It takes a very strong sense of safety and empowerment to be ready to face a potential tsunami of emotions like powerlessness when the defensive barrier is breached, especially since it was those very emotions that necessitated the defenses in the first place.

The overwhelming sense of unsafety which is the hall-mark of psychological trauma keeps defense mechanisms in place. Though they help sufferers negotiate daily life, they do interfere with genuine encounter with others. Our need for a sense of safety in order to enjoy being emotionally close to another human being is indicative of our connection with the animal world: "The natural state of mammals is to be somewhat on guard. However, in order to feel emotionally close to another human being our defensive system must temporarily shut down. In order to play, mate, and nurture our young, the brain needs to turn off its natural vigilance."[32] However, if the defensive system will not shut down, even temporarily, heartfelt connection in relationships becomes all but impossible.

RELATIONSHIPS

Because no relationship is more important than our relationship with God, this section will be our bridge to a Christian response to trauma and abuse. Life-diminishing disconnections between self and body, and thought and emotion—not to mention self and other people—leaves a person feeling alone in a desolate, colorless world which has lost the meaning that our Creator wishes to bestow on us through emotional awareness and relationships. Even meeting someone's eyes in a simple social encounter can arouse fear.[33] The life of the trauma victim with the scaffolding of defense mechanisms still in place is more often than not scarred by failed attempts at relationships and trapped in a lifetime of friendless solitary confinement. "You don't need a history of trauma to feel self-conscious and even panicked at a party with strangers—but trauma can turn the whole world into a gathering of aliens."[34] Imagine what this social hypervigilance does to a survivor who attends a church gathering.

Deeper still, the defenses that protect the victim from the unbearable reality of trauma are also self-alienating. The sensory self which knows the truth of what happened has to be silenced, along with the emotions, in order to perpetuate the defensive lie that the trauma did not actually happen. Survivors are never lonelier than when they are alone with themselves, since the self refuses, or is unable, to listen to the truth of her or his embodied reality. There is a part of the traumatized that knows the truth, whatever defenses might insist to the contrary. We will call this the "truth-bearer," which in the traumatized is often silenced by defenses. As Benner comments:

> Chasms that often exist between the truth of our being and the lies we live become major fault lines in our souls. No longer aligned with our center, we are forced to live from the periphery of our self. However, cut off from the taproot of our integrity and the truth of our existence, the distance between the truth of our being and the lies of our lives increases as we spiral into an abyss of pretense and nonpresence.

Is it any wonder that in this place of pretense, genuine presence is so impossible to achieve? Until we can be present to ourselves, we can never be fully present to anything. Presence to anything starts with presence to ourselves. We can never hope to know the presence of God or other people until we can be with ourselves in stillness, openness, and attentiveness. Presence to anything starts with presence to the only self through which we can ever know presence—our own.[35]

It is important not to misunderstand what is being said here. Benner is not saying that God refuses to be present to us unless we are still, open, and attentive as though God were requiring an exercise in religious meditation as a condition for his presence to us. We must understand what it means to be present to ourselves. We can be present to others physically when we are not present personally, for example, when we do not or cannot attend to anything that they are saying. By analogy, we are present to ourselves when we are attending to ourselves, in touch with ourselves, open, as it were, to ourselves. Most of us probably think we are naturally present to ourselves in that way without even being conscious of it. It is a substratum of our being, taken for granted. As a matter of fact, we frequently deceive ourselves, but, more to the point, this sense of presence to ourselves can be compromised by the psychological impact of trauma.

How can we become present to ourselves? A focus of mind and spirit is necessary. To become present involves a degree of inner stillness where we stop running from anyone or anything in either our external or internal world. "Where are you?" God called to Adam in the garden. True presence to ourselves means that we stop hiding, whether because of shame or distrust, or false pretenses about ourselves. If we are not present to ourselves, not really "at home," we will miss the presence of others altogether. We must be prepared to accept the reality of presence, open to the unexpectedness of our own or another's true being, and willing to give our attention actively to the one whose presence we seek, whether our own or another's. We underline the point that we are talking here about our capacity as humans to experience presence and not about some precondition which God asks us to meet before he will listen to our prayer. That is what we mean when we say that our experience of presence, whether to ourselves or others or God, entails some degree of stillness, openness, and attentiveness, however minimal, however fleeting. Only then can we have the quality of attention that can register the reality of that presence, including that of God.[36]

When missing in parent-child interactions, a lack of presence makes a substantial difference to the child's feeling of security and capacity for developing his or her own sense of presence. Emotional deprivation is a lack of presence to the emotional communication of the child, which leaves him or her with persistent feelings of utter isolation. In the traumatized, there are enduring obstacles to this receptive awareness, particularly the terror that shuts off awareness to anything or anyone other than the threat. Significant parts of the self are locked behind defenses that prevent those parts from participating in the relational dynamic of presence. This obviously has religious significance. When defenses block the capacity for self-presence in the traumatized, then the traumatized self cannot be present to God in the sense that we have explicated, and the experience of God's presence is obstructed.

The presence of God is particularly problematic for those who are inwardly divided by defenses. In its nature, our relationship with God is unlike our relationship with anyone or anything else. God is not a frail and limited creature, but Lord of heaven and earth. Yet when individuals relate to him, they relate in all their individuality and peculiarity. God does not abolish our differences from each other but begins in us, as we are, a work of transformation that he brings to completion beyond the grave. In our fallen world, our physical, psychological, and emotional condition affects our relationship with him from our end. Those defenses given to us by God for short-term survival can in the longer term keep out Light and Love himself as far as the survivor's developed conscious awareness is concerned, as though we were damming the flow of the river of Life, which is for the healing of the nations and their individual members (Rev 22:1).

It goes without saying that we are not casting spiritual blame on victims for this outcome any more than we blame them for being victims in the first place. It is a tragedy that the consequences of trauma that stand in the way of healthy relationships with others impact, *from the side of the survivor,* the relationship with God. Although the traumatized sometimes testify to intense spiritual experiences,[37] commonly the immediate impact of posttraumatic emotional overload is to eclipse our sense of the presence of God. Many who have never suffered abuse experience his painful absence in moments of intense grief. In the case of the traumatized, however, a more enduring sense of absence becomes a disabling structural feature of their internal world where the sense of the reality of God's presence is at best intermittent. Dissociation leaves the traumatized self feeling disowned and shunned, imprisoned in isolation, not present to anyone, and with no one present to that self. Where people in this situation also believe in God, two belief systems can function in conflict side by side. For instance, they believe *both* that Christ has gained access for them into God's presence through the cross *and* that God would never want to be close to their inner reality in what they perceive to be its shameful weakness.

Traumatized people find it hard to know where truth lies since the defensive system seems to have its own self-evident validity. The effect of collision between Scripture and our defensive systems is evident in the posttraumatic theological reasoning of William Cowper, a victim of bullying and abuse shortly after the trauma of losing his beloved mother at the age of six. Many years later in a letter to John Newton, he wrote:

> They think it necessary to the existence of divine truth, that he who once had possession of it should never finally lose it. I admit the solidity of this reasoning in every case but my own. And why not in my own? ... I forestall the answer:—God's ways are mysterious, and He giveth no account of His matters. ... There is a mystery in my destruction, and in time it shall be explained.[38]

The struggle to acquire divine assurance of grace where the believer's inner voice says otherwise is familiar enough in the history of the church independently of any issues of trauma. Where there is trauma, defense structures create a sturdy barrier. Cowper believed theologically in the perseverance of the saints, but the belief had no purchase on his experience.[39] Sadly, the experience of God and his graciously loving presence became increasingly inaccessible to him.

When posttraumatic emotions are not dealt with by safe, understanding responses at the time of the trauma, they are exacerbated by a wound of shameful helplessness, particularly with childhood trauma. "Why," the person might ask, "can I not cope with my overwhelming feelings if not because there is something dreadfully wrong with me?" Or, "Am I just too messed up to be understood? Or too reprehensible or repugnant to be comforted?" When unresolved emotions are cellared beneath powerful defensive structures that sustain the traumatized but keep them largely ignorant of the cause of their emotions, then secret, profound shame of distressing emotions saturates the sufferer. Trapped in inner powerlessness, despite any meticulously constructed outward façade of normality, the traumatized are often terrified that this secret shame will be found out. Real intimacy then becomes even more impossible and the prospect of it a threat. This applies to the relationship with God as well.

In Galatians 5:22, Paul describes the fruit of the Spirit. We later address briefly the question of the Spirit's work in the traumatized but let us at this point reflect on Paul's list in light of the fact that Scripture views the path to holiness in terms of growth and perseverance, not of leap and instant arrival. Yet trauma can blight spiritual fruit; this can be still another source of shame. The autonomic defenses that we described earlier, as well as powerful unprocessed posttraumatic emotions, compromise a capacity for self-control. Gentleness and kindness presuppose an awareness of others that is often beyond the reach of someone overwhelmed by the active volcanoes marking the posttraumatic inner life. Faithfulness assumes a capacity for consistency. The irritability that is a hallmark of trauma militates against patience. Lack of any sense of safety makes life as peaceful as walking on thin ice. The bloom of joy, which has roots in hope, withers when hope is uprooted like a tree (Job 19:10). Love formed in the traumatized person is often narcissistic, like that of a child, because emotions have not been processed with higher levels of emotional reasoning and the inexorable consciousness of acute pain turns awareness inward. All of this breeds discouragement and shame when the traumatized encounters Paul's description of life in the Spirit.

The fear of trusting which already blocks the way to intimacy is heightened by shame, sending the sufferer into hiding behind a false self that further hinders a sense of God's presence.

> As long as we ourselves are real, as long as we are truly ourselves, God can be present and can do something with us. But the moment we try to be what we are not, there is nothing left to say or have; we become a fictitious personality, an unreal presence, and this unreal presence cannot be approached by God.[40]

The word "cannot" in this last line has to be qualified or else, again, it will sound as though God is himself limited by our limitations, or that he puts the wrong kind of conditions on his promises to be present with us (Heb 13:5). We know that God can do all things. However, in sovereign freedom he also takes us as we are. If an abused or emotionally deprived child grows up with a pervasive sense of shame in his or her being, then that person's whole way of seeing, which has required the covering of defenses, must be gently approached with understanding and encountered on terms of mutual trust so as to open the way for this horrendous misunderstanding to be set right.

The word "cannot" needs further qualification in this context. Often the traumatized who cling to Christian faith agonizingly cry: "Why will God not immediately and supernaturally create in me a disposition to trust, abolishing my shame, renewing my whole inner being?" The question stands in continuity with questions often asked by the nontraumatized. This is not to reduce callously the experience of the traumatized to the dimensions of wider human experience. It is just to indicate that if we ask how we should answer the question on the part of the nontraumatized, it may help us to respond to it when it comes from the traumatized.

Our answer must surely be to distinguish between the realms of the personal and the impersonal. God can instantly turn water into wine, even if it is an exceptional action. God can instantly heal people of leprosy, even if that is exceptional too. Although the first action is directed to the nonpersonal world and the second to the human person, it is directed in the latter case to the physical dimension of the human being, so there is something in common between the two actions. But God's action in relation to human trust and shame is action in a different sphere. We rightly speak of a miracle of grace, of unbelief transformed into faith, despair into hope, hatred into love. Yet such transformation can occur very slowly over a period of time both as the Spirit puts us on the path to Jesus

Christ and as he leads us to sanctification in Jesus Christ. God treats water as water, and leprosy as leprosy, because that is what they are. He also treats persons as persons because that is who we are, and trust and shame reside in the deepest stratum of our personal being. We shall take this up briefly later as we ask more specifically about the Spirit, and now turn to the question of how we are to think biblically and faithfully about these things.

6

CHRISTIAN
REFLECTIONS

GOD MEANS CHRISTIANS to understand the workings of the body so that healing can come about through scientific knowledge even if he can bring it about without any human medical intervention. The meaning of the words "spirit," "soul," or "mind" and how these are connected with the body has long been a subject of theological discussion, but whatever they are and however connected, they do not exist in a self-enclosed, disembodied space. While we are in this world we are in the body, and even beyond this world Scripture does not portray a disembodied existence. Of course, we rightly distinguish the physical and the spiritual for certain purposes. We are not wrong to distinguish in terms of the physical and the spiritual between a broken arm and a state of being consumed by envy. But where trauma and abuse are involved, the spirit is affected by the body and the body by the spirit, and what is central to all humans, the brain, which is a physical organism, participates in both realms.

Before saying anything further, we underline how deep and fundamental is the biblical summons for us to love one another. Love is deeply penetrating and discriminating. Of course, its insight is not infallible. However, as we seek a loving understanding of people, we are aware of limits, kinds, and degrees of responsibility: for one, they seem to be responsible; for another, they do not seem to be responsible; for a third, they seem to be partly responsible. Scripture affords us the space to reflect and interact with others in their individuality, best we can.

At the heart of the church's response to the abused must be not only love but, as its expression, the creation of space for their stories to be told. This has to happen if traumatic emotions are to be processed and integrated into faith. Even if initial communication is simply, for instance, through the tightening of the throat, chest, or gut, or perhaps groans and sighs, these expressions of the body need to be translated gradually into words that can express the feelings they convey, whether with help or on one's own. This is part and parcel of emotional processing.

But great care must be taken not to forge ahead of the storyteller. The narrative should be allowed to grow spontaneously in the safe soil of true presence as the body develops the capacity safely to confront and communicate its own version of its experience in its own time. True presence is always predominantly concerned with the ongoing, in-the-moment well-being of the other, rather than any other goals of its own, however therapeutic.[41] Although far from easy, given a safe storytelling space, the unspeakable gradually becomes speakable, however much words inadequately represent experience. Eventually, a story can emerge that adequately captures the reality of the person's experience. As Jesus himself models for us in Mark 5:33 (in its context), making a safe space for story is key to the healing which makes the intimacy of indwelling faith possible.

Scripture extols truthful speech, and retelling the story can help the traumatized tell it more truthfully. "The fundamental premise of the psychotherapeutic work is a belief in the restorative power of truth-telling."[42] A fuller account of the narrative process cannot be explored within the confines of this article. Suffice it to say that the traumatized believer who desires healing in all its dimensions, including the spiritual, will ultimately need an adequately faithful and coherent story that represents *both* the experience of trauma *and* the story of God's love in Jesus Christ, incorporating the struggles to see and believe in that love in his or her own experience of suffering and evil. Experience of trauma is most truthfully narrated through the eyes and moment-by-moment embodied awareness of the experiencer.[43] What ultimately helps the traumatized is not primarily to be asked to give a logically ordered account observable from the outside, but to narrate a moment-by-moment awareness from the inside of the experience. He or she thus gives a uniquely personal map of his or her experience, which arises out of and contributes further to self-understanding.[44] This is not a subjective philosophical construction of truth; rather, it lays bare the personal data of experience on which the light of the gospel must shine. When the storyteller can recognize her or his experience in this story and feel that the account adequately contains that experience, then the traumatized is prepared for the transforming work of Jesus in that traumatic reality.

Stories are a vital means of understanding ourselves and others. Many whose identities have been formed in security take the sense of their own selves for granted as they navigate their way through the world. They may be able to "tell the story" of their lives or experiences relatively easily. However, if our defenses disable our capacity to access key truths of our experience, then we will not be able to develop a coherent representation of our lives, thwarting a crucial source of self-understanding and what we might call "self-indwelling"—the unconscious sense of our own unity.[45] This not only leaves us with a fragmented sense of self, lacking a core sense of agency, but also clutters up the space in our hearts in which the Spirit seeks to dwell. The Spirit is the sovereign Lord of grace and love but wills that we be receptive.

Denial, avoidance, dissociation, and idealization, along with all the factors that made them necessary, need to come to light. Of course, this is often a professional responsibility, particularly because of the difficulty of constructing a trauma narrative, where coherent storying (so crucial for a whole sense of self) founders on the overwhelming threat posed by the traumatic reality represented in the trauma narrative. But just as mutual pastoral care must take place in congregations even though minister and elders have a peculiar pastoral responsibility, so members of a congregation can create a space for safety and openness even when there is specialized counseling or therapeutic work to be done. Where a story can be told and properly heard, the reality experienced in our bodies can come out of hiding into the light of words. Then we can bring the hidden needs to the One who can bind up broken hearts, so that the truthful story of the living God can truly touch the unique personal truth of our stories. True prayer becomes possible. In the words of C. S. Lewis:

> And in prayer this real I struggles to speak, for once, from his real being. … The attempt is not to escape from space and time and from my creaturely situation. … It is more modest: to reawaken the awareness of that situation. If that can be done, there is no need to go anywhere else. This situation itself, is, at every moment, a possible theophany.[46] Here is the Holy Ground. The Bush is burning now. …. The prayer preceding all prayers is, "May it be the real I who speaks. May it be the real Thou that I speak to."[47]

We do not have to subscribe to everything in this formulation (we might want to avoid the dramatic connotations of "theophany") in order to appreciate the importance of the point being made. Telling our own story to God makes our prayer more honest; with this truthful speaking to God begins the restoration of our sense of responsibility before him. Bringing the real self before the real God is the first step in taking our God-given responsibility before him.

When I put my painful traumatic experience into words and bring them to the Lord in prayer, I open the door of my inner reality to my heavenly Father. Taking responsibility means I am no longer waiting passively for God to heal me instantly and supernaturally or assuming that because he knows me I do not need actively to bring my personal reality to him.

"Though the survivor is not responsible for the injury that was done to her, she is responsible for her recovery."[48] It seems unjust that the sufferer bears responsibility for rebuilding what has been torn down. Paradoxically, while it appears to be unjust to have to take responsibility for our situation, it turns out to be empowering in the good sense of that word. "The only way that the survivor can take full control of her recovery is to take responsibility for it. The only way she can discover her undestroyed strengths is to use them to their fullest."[49] Similarly, the owner of a store whose shop is bombed is nonetheless responsible for facing the task of cleaning it up. You alone can and must face your pain and mourn your losses, but that does not mean doing it alone. Help with healing comes through extending ourselves in relationship, actively opening ourselves to and receiving the benefits of that relationship. The sooner this responsibility is accepted, the sooner the task of restoration will be accomplished, however long that may turn out to be.

Obviously, the process of restoring a sense of agency in the context of radical powerlessness means that the body of Christ assumes responsibility where utterly broken individuals cannot fend for themselves. This does not perpetuate but rather transforms the brokenness, aiming for the maturity of each believer by helping to restore the sense of agency so fundamental for that maturity. When churches enable stories to be told, then traumatized survivors of abuse begin to acquire a sense of responsibility. This is profoundly the will of God for his people. The church lives in the light of a long-term prospect—it is a pilgrim people seeking a heavenly city, and we encourage each other to persevere. Truth-telling, prayer, love, and responsibility mark its life. The devil wants to turn our righteous sense of victimhood and experience of intense suffering into a stronghold against God's living word, summoning us to responsibility. Our suffering is something ultimately to be included as we offer our lives to God as living sacrifices.

Submission to God's authority is crucial in order to rebuild the sense of agency and an appropriate sense of authority lost in the overwhelming powerlessness of trauma. Of course, we must distinguish between actions that characterize the internal relationship between God the Father and God the Son and those that are appropriate for humans before God. Nonetheless, we must ponder the implications for our own God-given responsibility of how God gave the Son, who was utterly submissive to his Father's authority, the authority to take up and lay down his life (John 10:17–18). There is no contradiction between God's gift of authority to the Son and the Son's assignment to himself of authority.[50] Nor is there contradiction when

Scripture exhorts us to cleanse ourselves and purify our hearts of sin (2 Cor 7:1; 2 Tim 2:21; Jas 4:8). By authorizing us through his commands, God gives us "authority" in those things he authorizes us to do. Where the sense of responsibility and authorization comes naturally to those who have lived secure lives—they usually do not even notice or take account of it—it comes as a sense of "authority" when radically disempowered trauma survivors are enabled to develop that sense and receive a sense of agency.

Jesus' acts of obedience and authority alike mirrored his Father's indwelling; in fact, they constituted a sustained unity with the Father. This is the Christ whom we are invited to indwell and who promises to make his home in us (John 14:20). He wants to indwell the terrified, utterly alone, disempowered, and broken self that bears the shame of victimization, even when those who suffer cannot be sure that they are experiencing him. In a different sense, we must indwell the stories—however incoherently they are told—through our listening to those who are terrified, utterly alone, disempowered, and broken, doing so, for example, through our lament on their behalf that cries out for the eschatological new creation. Martin Luther, the greatest postbiblical defender of justification by faith alone in the history of the Christian church said: "The Christian lives in Christ and in his neighbor. Otherwise he is not a Christian. He indwells Christ through faith and his neighbor through love."[51] Through his people, God makes his appeal of reconciliation to disowned selves disconnected from their own core personality, imprisoned behind an unseen wall of defenses that makes them also invisible. We share with the abused the message of reconciliation to a God who created a world subsequently broken by sin and alienation and who longs to rescue the vulnerable, shunned part of the self which has never been properly seen, much less been the subject of indwelling.

As God heard and responded to the one who went to the cross where God and world were reconciled, so he also listens and responds to our laments even when they are not purified as Christ is pure, however angry or beleaguered they are. Before God, lament

> is an act of bold faith, albeit a transformed faith, because it insists that the world must be experienced as it really is. ... All such experiences of disorder are a proper subject for discourse with God. ... Everything properly belongs in this conversation of the heart. To withhold part of life from that conversation is in fact to withhold part of life from the sovereignty of God.[52]

> Lament is a beginning point on the road to healing insofar as it enables us to move from silence into a mode of speech that is potentially healing and transformative. The act of lament is radical because it refuses to acknowledge the hopelessness and nihilism through which western culture views evil, suffering, and death.[53]

Our New Testament is integrated into a Scripture which gives lament its place, conspicuously in Job and the Psalms. Lament is a truthful place to start, both "identifying the truth of an experience [that] is essential to healing from trauma"[54] and acknowledging the reality of a faithful God who would indwell us in the places that previously felt godforsaken. Truth opens the way to life. Recovery and restoration may seem insuperable targets for the trauma survivor, but the promise of new creation in Christ goes beyond clinical recovery from and restoration after trauma. Nothing less than the God's new creation at the end of time will bring complete healing.

Should we speak of victory as well as lament in relation to the traumatized? Those who are conversant with trauma, either directly or through counseling, find that healing from trauma can last a lifetime. Does this collide with the apostolic confidence that the fullness of the Spirit enables the fruit of the Spirit to grow abundantly? Do Paul and his fellow-apostles, on the one hand, think in religious and moral categories so that religious and moral transformation is possible through the Holy Spirit while, on the other hand, our discussion hitherto has employed clinical categories and, on that basis, talked in terms of the long haul? There is no collision. The biblical and experiential worlds may be brought together in at least two ways.

First, in the history of Christian theology, there have been different ways of understanding theologically the nature and extent of the Holy Spirit's work. Does Romans 7 describe ongoing Christian experience that we should expect to remain ours in all its force in this world, or does Paul summon us to move on from Romans 7 to victory in Romans 8? Are we to understand the revivals that have punctuated the life of Christian churches as extraordinary operations that do not characterize mundane life in the Spirit, or as signs of how God would have his people experience him much of or all the time, if they are obedient? We shall not here rivet our attempt to respond from a Christian point of view to trauma and abuse to one particular interpretation of the work of the Spirit which is controversial in the Christian church. However, it is surely the case that the New Testament authors envision a power at work within us, as a church and as individuals, which is greater than what we often experience or settle for. If this is so, then the lack of spiritual power in many of our churches and in ourselves as individual Christians surely contribute to the slowness of the pace of progress and recovery in traumatized members. Reflection on the spiritual misery of trauma stimulates reflection on the spiritual poverty of so many churches and Christian lives. As authors, we do not regard ourselves as having transcended this condition.

Secondly, Scripture combines a wonderfully exalted view of the Spirit's work and power with a liberating realism about life in the Christian fellowship. Paul and his fellow apostles know that there are the weak and the strong, those who regularly fail and those who firmly stand, the immature and the mature. They are all in the church. God did not need to give to the biblical authors a knowledge of the physiological mechanism of trauma more than he gave Luke knowledge of third-millennium medicine, but his inspired word opens up the space for the self-understanding of future generations. The apostles collectively instruct us to be gentle, discerning, truthful, and hopeful. Just as he does not give all the same gifts, so the Holy Spirit does not work in exactly the same way at exactly the same pace in every individual believer or in those who will come to faith. We must always remember that Paul's letters included in the New Testament are usually written not to individuals but to churches, and not everything in every epistle will apply to every person in exactly the same way at every moment, as any preacher knows who speaks in specific ways to a very diverse congregation. Indeed, those who bore Paul's letters to faraway congregations would have explained and applied their content in more or less detail as the particular and various circumstances required. Biblical depiction of life in the Spirit and clinical depiction of recovery from trauma may appear to collide in certain respects but are consonant in the depths when we observe both the power and patience Paul and others embodied in the name of Father, Son, and Spirit.

The fallen condition is one of separation; the healed condition is one of unification. God can use evil in unanticipated ways. For instance, like the other defenses, DID is a gift from God to cope with the extreme fallout of a fallen world, much as he stitched skins for Adam and Eve (Gen 3:21). However, all perpetuated defenses ultimately divide the self in different ways, though DID does this structurally. Separation is the goal of the evil one: the separation of the self from God; separation from neighbor, and, thus, the inward disintegration of the human individual in order to separate self from self as far as that is metaphysically possible. God's creation introduces distinction—for the first time, something other than God exists. Satan is incapable of creation, but he can entice humans to relate to creation without relating properly to their Creator. Thus he aims at the separation of humans from their Creator which is at the root of their alienation from each other and of their inward disintegration as individuals. God, however, wills both communion with the humans whom he has made and harmony in human relationships; and his design for us as individuals is that reason, emotion, will, conscience, and spirit should be integrated in our bodily existence here on earth.[55] Redemption is at the very least reclamation of the creation order.

Just as the Old Testament places Israel at the center of God's election and purposes, so the New places the church there. It is the place where healing for the traumatized and abused is to take place. Early in the history of the church, the parable of the Good Samaritan was interpreted in terms of Jesus Christ as the Samaritan and the church as the inn to which he brought the wounded traveler to convalesce and be refreshed.[56] We may not want to interpret the parable allegorically, but an important point is made when the church is identified as a place of convalescence. The church is much more than this, and if we were to make the convalescent home a governing ecclesiological image, we should marginalize without warrant much of what is said about the church in the New Testament. But while we are on the pilgrimage of life, we are also convalescents, and none will feel this more keenly than the abused and traumatized in the worshiping congregation. Sadly, for far too many people, the church has been a place of abuse rather than of safety.

The challenge for the church is to be both emotionally and spiritually safe for convalescents from abuse. This requires both emotional and spiritual maturity, with all the courage this entails to face unprocessed emotions as well as the darkest realities of this fallen world in the safe presence of an eternally safe Father. These are the realities in which we are called to be his body, to dwell in the furthest outposts of human experience in the Spirit of Jesus. Emotional and spiritual maturity are interdependent: you cannot be truly mature spiritually without emotional maturity any more than you can be truly emotionally mature without spiritual maturity.[57] Both are vital for a safe emotional and spiritual environment for healing. Any lack of safety that prevents reunification or integration of those divided by defenses will be co-opted by the evil one who relishes any division. We need to put emotionally healthy, truly loving relationships at the heart of the church's notion of discipleship, because the likely outcome of failure to do so would be that people both inside and outside the churches will believe that Christian truth is not life-transforming and even potentially damaging.

The extent of victory in these circumstances, as in the Christian life more generally, may be far greater than what we normally imagine. However, the persistence of struggle will also be greater than those who have not experienced trauma can normally imagine. For the traumatized, victory begins when the shame and terror of their trauma, with all the emotionally held beliefs associated with them, become exposed to God's truth and love. The cleansing power of God's truth disinfects the wound from the distortions and lies acquired in the traumatic experience, while God's love makes his truth lifegiving. The awesome reality of God can meet and touch the deepest existential reality of the traumatized, opening doors to God's presence so that his reality is increasingly experienced in the here and now while the traumatic events are increasingly experienced as part of the past. This is never an isolated journey. In this article, as we have sought to understand trauma and abuse and to think theologically about them, we have always kept in mind that it is "through the church" that "the manifold wisdom of God" is "made known to the rulers and authorities in the heavenly places" (Eph 3:10).

We conclude, however, not with the church but with him who is our Wisdom, a wisdom scandalously portrayed and preached in the gospel of the cross (1 Cor 1:17–2:2). We have frequently alluded to shame in the traumatized. Shame is deep, pervasive, and often concealed in human

75

life quite generally. Where it is felt, its roots, nature, and reason are nevertheless hidden. No anti-Christian philosopher in the West has been more influential than Friedrich Nietzsche, who closes the third "book" of the work usually translated under the title *The Gay Science* with eight questions. The last three are these: "*Whom do you call bad?*—He who always wants to put people to shame. *What is most human to you?*—To spare someone shame. *What is the seal of having become free?*—No longer to be ashamed before oneself."[58] For Nietzsche, Christianity was depraved on many counts, but on no account greater than its insistence that humans should be ashamed of themselves. A true son of Adam, Nietzsche, like the rest of us, was hiding.[59]

A popular Christian song includes the line: "You took all my sin and shame when you died and rose again." In our theologies of the atonement, we have developed our thought much more in relation to how Jesus Christ bore our sin than how he took our shame. Given the surface of the biblical witness to the atoning death of Jesus Christ, that is natural. Nor shall we to try to foist on readers of this article in a closing paragraph a theology of the atonement in relation to shame. However, biblical scholars, like social and anthropological commentators, often emphasize the "shame-honor" culture or cultures that characterized ancient Near Eastern society and characterizes Near and East Asian societies (for example) in our own day. Jesus Christ, hanging bloody and disrobed on the cross, was an extremely shameful spectacle.

In taking our sin upon himself, Christ came to the place where we are, the place of abandoned godforsakenness, pitch black under the cloud of divine judgment. He finds humans there in all their various kinds of shame as well as their guilt. He is the one who, as Isaiah 53 tells us, bore our griefs and carried our sorrows, upon whom was the chastisement that brought us peace. He bore the sin of transgressors and makes intercession for transgressors themselves. He did it in the form of one who had no desirable beauty, was despised and rejected, "as one from whom men hide their faces,"[60] crushed, oppressed, afflicted. If there is unfathomable depth in the way Jesus Christ bore the guilt of human sin, so there is surely an unfathomable reality in the way that he identified himself with the misery of human shame.

What that means for the abused and traumatized we shall not venture to suggest here.[61] It is in his company that they will learn what it means. We are on holy ground when we ask what it meant for the Son of God to enter into the experience of human shame in its bleakest, most painful forms. But the Jesus who was raised from the dead for the justification of the ungodly (Rom 3:25) joins to himself those who have been shamed and does so as one who knows and calls his sheep by name (John 10:3). In calling them by name, he knows all about them. In calling on his name, those who turn to him may know that name in all the beauty of the risen presence of the wounded and crucified Christ. As long as the church proclaims in both word and life the infinite depths of the mercy and suffering displayed and experienced in the Son of God on the cross, it will proclaim the greatest of all healing truths—that it is by the wounds of him who entered in solidarity into the condition of human sin and shame and rose again in victory that we are healed (Isa 53:5).

Acknowledgments

T HE SERIES Questions for Restless Minds is produced by the Christ on Campus Initiative, under the stewardship of the editorial board of D. A. Carson (senior editor), Douglas Sweeney, Graham Cole, Dana Harris, Thomas McCall, Geoffrey Fulkerson, and Scott Manetsch. The editorial board recognizes with gratitude the many outstanding evangelical authors who have contributed to this series, as well as the sponsorship of Trinity Evangelical Divinity School (Deerfield, Illinois), and the financial support of the MAC Foundation and the Carl F. H. Henry Center for Theological Understanding. The editors also wish to thank Christopher Gow, who created the study questions accompanying each book, and Todd Hains, our editor at Lexham Press. May God alone receive the glory for this endeavor!

Study Guide Questions

1. Have you ever thought of trauma as a psycho-spiritual phenomenon?

2. What about this account of the complexity trauma was new to you?

3. What do you think of this quote: "You cannot be truly mature spiritually without emotional maturity any more than you can be truly emotionally mature without spiritual maturity"?

4. What does this book teach us about the nature of sin and its effects?

5. What does it mean to be in touch with ourselves? What do the authors say about how this relates to our ability to be present to others? About our awareness of God's presence?

6. Are there any theological truths that you believe in general but are hard to accept as true for yourself? See Cowper's example, pages 52–53.

7. How does the article help you think about the kind of community that Christians should be?

8. Are there any ways that you need to "open the door of [your] inner reality to [your] heavenly Father" (66)? Maybe this would look like lament, confession, or thanksgiving. Spend some time this week journaling and praying in complete honesty and openness to God.

For Further Reading

UNDERSTANDING TRAUMA

Gerhardt, Sue. *Why Love Matters: How Affection Shapes a Baby's Brain*. Routledge, 2004.

> A non-technical book showing what happens when children don't get what they need to develop psychologically. Links the neuropsychological damage of emotional deprivation with the known impact of abuse.

Herman, Judith. *Trauma and Recovery: From Domestic Abuse to Political Terror*. HarperCollins, 1994.

> A trauma classic, charting the impact of trauma and providing a basic map for recovery. Covers such global catastrophes as war as well as personal catastrophes like sexual abuse.

Van der Kolk, Bessel. *The Body Keeps the Score: Brain, Mind, and Body in the Healing of Trauma.* Penguin, 2014.

This landmark guide by one of the most trusted names in traumatology details trauma's neuro-physiological impact. Helps the church not to over-spiritualize posttraumatic stress and to understand better the suffering of trauma survivors.

PERSONAL STORIES

Braddock Bromley, Nicole. *Hush: Moving from Silence to Healing after Childhood Sexual Abuse.* Moody, 2007.

Narrates both the author's story and stories of students to whom she ministered. Speaks directly to the issues with which many sexual abuse survivors in universities and colleges struggle.

Bramhall, Carolyn. *Am I a Good Girl Yet?: Childhood Abuse Had Shattered Her. Could She Ever Be Whole?* Monarch, 2005.

A victim of satanic abuse reveals the dissociative nightmare of extreme trauma. Her personal story of recovered faith and relationships shows that victims can recover.

CHURCH AND SPIRITUALITY

Benner, David. *Presence and Encounter: The Sacramental Possibilities of Everyday Life*. Brazos, 2014.

> An approach to wholeness in body, mind, and spirit showing how we can grow more connected in relationships with God, self, and others.

Wilder, James. *Living from the Heart Jesus Gave You*. Shepherd's Bush, 2013.

> A practical vision of how the church can be committed to the abused. Much godly wisdom on such things as boundaries and healthy relationships.

Notes

1. We are aware that the interpretation of this verse is contested.
2. T. S. Eliot, "Choruses from 'the Rock,'" https://www.arak29.am/PDF_PPT/6-Literature/Eliot/Chtherock_eng.htm.
3. Online Etymology Dictionary, https://www.etymonline.com/word/trauma.
4. See Bessel van der Kolk's account of the history of the neuroscience revolution in the late twentieth century in *The Body Keeps the Score: Brain, Mind, and Body in the Healing of Trauma* (Penguin, 2014), 39–47.
5. Van der Kolk, *The Body*, 142.
6. Although we sometimes use the word *victim* for those who experience trauma, the word *survivor* is usually preferred because it conveys respect for the active role of overcoming the painful psychospiritual consequences of trauma.

7. Meena Vythilingam et. al., "Childhood Trauma Associated with Smaller Hippocampal Volume in Women with Major Depression," *American Journal of Psychiatry*, 159 (2002): 2072–80.

8. There are specific subcategories that we will not mention here, such as domestic abuse, though we recognize their importance. See N. E. Nienhuis, "Theological reflections on violence and abuse," *Journal of Pastoral Care and Counseling* 59 (2005): 109–23.

9. https://www.gov.uk/government/collections/serious-crime-bill.

10. https://www.womensaid.org.uk/information-support/what-is-domestic-abuse/coercive-control/.

11. Van der Kolk, *The Body*, 87. Perhaps as many as six out of ten questions in the ACE study questionnaire relate to emotional abuse or neglect: "1. Did a parent or other adult in the household often … swear at you, insult you, put you down, or humiliate you? … 4. Did you often feel that … no one in your family loved you or thought you were important or special? or Your family didn't look out for each other, feel close to each other, or support each other? … 6. Were your parents ever separated or divorced? … 8. Did you live with anyone who was a problem drinker or alcoholic or who used street drugs? 9. Was a household member depressed or mentally ill or did a house-

hold member attempt suicide? 10. Did a household member go to prison?" While the other questions relate to physical and sexual abuse, the role of emotional abuse and neglect in childhood maltreatment is conspicuously recognized in this monumental study by the CDC in Atlanta.

12.   Van der Kolk, *The Body*, 157.

13.   Martin Teicher, "Scars That Won't Heal: The Neurobiology of Child Abuse," *Scientific American* 286 (2002): 3. See also Michael D. De Bellis and Abigail Zisk, "The Biological Effects of Childhood Trauma," *Child and Adolescent Psychiatric Clinics of North America* 23 (2014): 185–222.

14.   "Epigenetic" refers to changes in the way genes are expressed (without actual changes to the DNA itself) that can be inherited (See https://www.whatisepigenetics.com/fundamentals). "McGill researcher Moshe Szyf compared the epigenetic profiles of hundreds of children born into extreme ends of social privilege in the United Kingdom and measured the effects of child abuse on both groups. Differences in social class were associated with distinctly different epigenetic profiles, but abused children in both groups had in common specific modifications in seventy-three genes." Van der Kolk, *The Body*, 154.

15.   "The unfinished business of early life, the feelings of fear that you will be abandoned or rejected

which were at their most potent when you were a dependent child; feelings that were overwhelming and unmanageable without a parental regulator; feelings of rage that your parent did not help you to cope with particular feelings; many feelings that were held back because it was not safe to feel them whilst you were a child, so dependent on the parent to regulate you and keep you alive." Sue Gerhardt, *Why Love Matters: How Affection Shapes a Baby's Brain* (Routledge, 2004), 204.

16. Van der Kolk, *The Body*, 150.

17. Ronnie Janoff-Bulman, "Assumptive Worlds and the Stress of Traumatic Events: Applications of the Schema Construct," *Social Cognition* 7.2 (1989): 121.

18. B. A. van der Kolk, "The Body Keeps the Score," in Bessel A. van der Kolk, Alexander C. McFarlane, and Lars Weisaeth, eds., *Traumatic Stress: The Effects of Overwhelming Experience on Mind, Body and Society* (The Guilford, 1996), 219.

19. R. D. Lane et al., "The Levels of Emotional Awareness Scale: A Cognitive-Developmental Measure of Emotion," *Journal of Personality Assessment* 55 (1990): 124–34.

20. See Babette Rothschild, *The Body Remembers: The Psychophysiology of Trauma and Trauma Treatment* (Norton, 2000).

21. See Phebe Cramer, *Protecting the Self: Defense Mechanisms in Action* (New York: Guilford, 2006).

22. Gerhardt, *Why Love Matters*, 204.

23. Gerhardt, *Why Love Matters*, 205.

24. Bruno Bettelheim, *The Informed Heart* (Penguin, 1960), 114.

25. https://ritualabuse.us/ritualabuse/articles/report -of-the-ritual-abuse-task-force-los-angeles-county -commission-for-women/.

26. James G. Friesen, *Uncovering the Mystery of MPD* (Wipf and Stock, 1997), 96.

27. In July 29, 1985, the *Chicago Tribune* published an article entitled: "Satanism Haunts Tales of Child Sex Abuse," detailing at length contemporary allegations of child sexual abuse and SRA, "including the drinking of blood, cannibalism and the sacrificial murders of other children." Testimonies of therapists interviewing the children were ominous: "I think anybody who works in this area ought to carry a badge and wear a gun, and not have a family"; and "Good luck with your life. ... My car was blown up 10 days ago."

28. The authors are grateful to John Wyatt for his comments on this area.

29. James G. Friesen, *More Than Survivors: Conversations with Multiple-Personality Clients* (Here's Life, 1992), 11.

30. Introjection is a defense mechanism that works by internalizing attitudes or attributes of another person, often a person perceived as having more

power in a situation where an individual is experiencing powerlessness.

31. "Many people are conscious of an inner voice that provides a running monologue throughout the day and even into the night. Cheerful and supportive or negative and self-defeating, this internal chatter is referred to as self-talk." https://www.psychology today.com/gb/basics/self-talk.

32. Van der Kolk, *The Body*, 86.

33. "The most striking difference between normal controls and survivors of chronic trauma was in the activation of the prefrontal cortex (PFC) in response to a direct eye gaze. The PFC normally helps us to assess the person coming toward us and our mirror neurons help us to pick up his intentions. However, the subjects with PTSD [Post-traumatic Stress Disorder] did not activate any part of their frontal lobe, which means they could not muster any curiosity about the stranger. They just reacted with intense activation deep inside their emotional brains, in the primitive areas known as the Periaqueductal Gray, which generates startled, hypervigilant, cowering, and other self-protective behaviors. There was no activation of any part of the brain involved in social engagement. In response to being looked at they simply went into survival mode." Van der Kolk, *The Body*, 104.

34. Van der Kolk, *The Body*, 81.

35. David Benner, *Presence and Encounter: The Sacramental Possibilities of Everyday Life* (Brazos, 2014), 28.

36. This is essentially what is portrayed in C. S. Lewis's powerful work, *Till We Have Faces: A Myth Retold* (Bles, 1956).

37. See Donald Kalsched, *Trauma and the Soul: A Psycho-Spiritual Approach to Human Development and Its Interruption* (Routledge, 2013).

38. Ralph Griffiths, "Private Correspondence of William Cowper," *The Monthly Review, or, Literary Journal* 104 (May–Aug, 1824): 179–180.

39. "Perseverance of the saints" is a theological phrase whose meaning is that those who truly put their faith in Jesus Christ for salvation will not lose that salvation because, although they often fail and fall, God will keep them to the end.

40. Metropolitan Anthony of Sourozh, *School for Prayer* (Darton, Longman & Todd, 1970), 30.

41. The authors are grateful to Richard Averbeck for his comments on the surrounding issues.

42. Judith Herman, *Trauma and Recovery: From Domestic Abuse to Political Terror* (HarperCollins, 1994), 181.

43. See Susan Lecky Williams, "Recovering from the Psychological Impact of Intensive Care: How Constructing a Story Helps," *Nursing in Critical Care* 14

(2009): 281–8; and *Life after a Critical Event in Hospital: An Exploration into the Language of Trauma* (Lambert Academic, 2010).

44. In fact, we are all dependent upon narrative as one of the "symbolic mediations" of self-understanding, since we cannot know ourselves directly. Self-knowledge is something we must work on. "The refiguration by narrative confirms this aspect of self-knowledge which goes far beyond the narrative domain, namely, that the self does not know itself immediately, but only indirectly by the detour of the cultural signs of all sorts which are articulated on the symbolic mediations which always already articulate action and, among them, the narratives of everyday life." Paul Ricoeur, "Narrative Identity," in David Wood, ed., *On Paul Ricoeur: Narrative and Interpretation* (Routledge, 2002), 198. Calvin announced that "Our wisdom, in so far as it ought to be deemed true and solid Wisdom, consists almost entirely of two parts: the knowledge of God and of ourselves," *Institutes of the Christian Religion*, trans. Ford Lewis Battles (SCM, 1961), 1.1.1.

45. Or what Winnicott calls *unit status* in D. W. Winnicott, "The Theory of the Parent-Infant Relationship," *International Journal of Psycho-Analysis* 41 (1960): 589: "The result of healthy progress in the infant's development ... is that he attains to what

might be called 'unit status.' The infant becomes a person, an individual in his own right. Associated with this attainment is the infant's psychosomatic existence, which begins to take on a personal pattern; I have referred to this as the psyche indwelling in the soma." When developmental trauma interferes with this profoundest docking of self with body, then the person's actual experience of the deep indwelling of Jesus is correspondingly attenuated. Already the person has an experiential handicap in faith.

46. "Theophany" literally means "an appearance of God" and usually refers to a distinct and dramatic experience of God such as that of Moses at the burning bush. Although Lewis refers here to that incident, he is deliberately using the dramatic word "theophany" simply to indicate a definite experience of God.

47. C. S. Lewis, *Letters to Malcolm: Chiefly on Prayer* (Bles, 1964), 108–09.

48. Herman, *Trauma and Recovery*, 133.

49. Herman, *Trauma and Recovery*, 192.

50. It is less important (though not unimportant) to elaborate this with theological precision than to accept the fact of it.

51. Martin Luther, "The Freedom of the Christian," *Luther's Works*, vol. 31 (Muhlenberg, 1957), 371, translation slightly altered. Of course, here we

are collapsing Christ's indwelling of us and our indwelling of him.

52. Walter Brueggemann, *The Message of the Psalms: A Theological Commentary* (Fortress, 1984), 52: "The reason the darkness may be faced and lived in is that even in the darkness, there is One to address. The One to address is in the darkness but is not simply a part of the darkness (John 1:1–5). Because this One has promised to be in the darkness with us, we find the darkness strangely transformed, not by the power of easy light, but by the power of relentless solidarity."

53. John Swinton, *Raging with Compassion: Pastoral Responses to the Problem of Evil* (Eerdmans, 2007), 130.

54. Van der Kolk, *The Body,* 355.

55. In a different way, God also purposes the harmony of humankind and the nonhuman creation.

56. See Origen, "Homily 34," in *Homilies on Luke*, trans. Joseph T. Lienhard (Catholic University of America, 1996). Origen is reporting on others' interpretations, as well as advancing his own interpretation in this homily.

57. See Peter Scazzero, *Emotionally Healthy Spirituality: It's Impossible to Be Spiritually Mature, While Remaining Emotionally Immature* (Zondervan, 2006).

58. Friedrich Nietzsche, *The Gay Science*, trans. Josefine Nauckhoff (Cambridge University Press, 2001), 152–53.

59. We do not here go into the distinction between healthy shame (which sees behavior as shameful/inappropriate) and toxic shame (which sees the self as shameful/defective).

60. Or "as one who hides his face from us" (Isa 53:3 ESV).

61. The following books can help the reader to explore the subject of shame. However, the posttraumatic defenses which block access not only to a sufferer's emotional awareness but sometimes even to his or her personal story are not dealt with in these books. Nonetheless, there is much that is helpful. Curt Thompson, *The Soul of Shame: Retelling the Stories We Believe about Ourselves* (IVP, 2015); Heather Davis Nelson, *Unashamed: Healing Our Brokenness and Finding Freedom from Shame* (Crossway, 2016); Edward T Welch, *Shame Interrupted: How God Lifts the Pain of Worthlessness and Rejection* (New Growth, 2012).